Martin Luther King Jr. Day

by Marc Tyler Nobleman

Content Adviser: Alton Hornsby Jr., Ph.D.,
Fuller E. Callaway Professor of History, Morehouse College, Atlanta, Georgia

Reading Adviser: Susan Kesselring, M.A., Literacy Educator,
Rosemount-Apple Valley-Eagan (Minnesota) School District

Let's See Library
Compass Point Books
Minneapolis, Minnesota

Compass Point Books
3109 West 50th Street, #115
Minneapolis, MN 55410

Visit Compass Point Books on the Internet at *www.compasspointbooks.com*
or e-mail your request to *custserv@compasspointbooks.com*

On the cover: Dr. Martin Luther King Jr. waves to people in a civil rights march in
Washington, D.C., on August 28, 1963.

Photographs ©: Bettmann/Corbis, cover; Howard Sochurek/Time Life Pictures/Getty Images, 4; Robert W.
Kelley/Time Life Pictures/Getty Images, 6; Hulton/Archive by Getty Images, 8; Erik S. Lesser/Getty Images,
10, 14; Diana Walker/Time Life Pictures/Getty Images, 12; Jim Whitmer Photography, 16; AP/World Wide
Photos, 18; Skjold Photographs, 20.

Creative Director: Terri Foley
Managing Editor: Catherine Neitge
Editors: Brenda Haugen and Christianne Jones
Photo Researcher: Marcie C. Spence
Designers: Melissa Kes and Les Tranby
Educational Consultant: Diane Smolinski

Library of Congress Cataloging-in-Publication Data
Nobleman, Marc Tyler.
    Martin Luther King Jr. Day / by Marc Tyler Nobleman.
       p. cm. — (Let's see)
    Includes bibliographical references and index.
    ISBN 0-7565-0646-8
1. Martin Luther King Jr. Day—Juvenile literature. 2. King, Martin Luther, Jr., 1929-1968—Juvenile
literature. [1. Martin Luther King, Jr. Day. 2. King, Martin Luther, Jr.] I. Title. II. Series.
E186.97.K5N63 2004
394.261—dc22   2003022179

Table of Contents

What Is Martin Luther King Jr. Day? 5

What Did Martin Luther King Jr. Do? 7

How Did Martin Luther King Jr. Change the U.S.? 9

Who Worked to Make the Holiday? 11

Did Everyone Like the New Holiday? 13

How Is Martin Luther King Jr. Day Observed? 15

Where Is Martin Luther King Jr. Day Observed? 17

What Is Special About Martin Luther King Jr. Day? 19

What Does the Holiday Mean to People? 21

Glossary 22
Did You Know? 22
Want to Know More? 23
Index 24

*NOTE: In this book, words that are defined in the glossary
are in **bold** the first time they appear in the text.*

What Is Martin Luther King Jr. Day?

Martin Luther King Jr. Day is an American holiday. It honors Dr. Martin Luther King Jr. He was a Baptist minister and a leader in the **civil rights movement.**

Dr. King worked hard to stop **racism.** Racism is judging people unfairly or treating people badly because of their skin color.

Martin Luther King Jr. Day is on the third Monday in January. The holiday is close to Dr. King's birthday. He was born January 15, 1929, in Atlanta, Georgia.

Martin Luther King Jr. Day is a time to remember all the things Dr. King did. It is also a time to follow his example and help others.

◄ *Dr. Martin Luther King Jr.*

What Did Martin Luther King Jr. Do?

Dr. King's life was full of brave actions. In 1955, he helped to stop **segregation** on public buses in Montgomery, Alabama.

Under segregation, black people could only sit in the back of a bus. However, if a white person wanted that seat, the black person would have to move. Dr. King and other black people chose not to ride any bus until the segregation stopped. In 1956, the United States Supreme Court said blacks could sit anywhere they wanted on a bus.

Dr. King kept working to end **discrimination.** He wanted all people to have equal rights, no matter the color of their skin.

◄ Dr. King helps lead a march for jobs and freedom in Washington, D.C.

How Did Martin Luther King Jr. Change the U.S.?

For a long time in the United States, black people did not have as many rights as white people. In some places, blacks were forced to use separate bathrooms and go to different schools. The schools the black children went to were usually not as nice as the ones white children attended.

Dr. King knew black people could make the country change. He said the change could happen without using violence. People thought Dr. King was a good man and took his advice. He helped blacks work together to win equality.

◄ *A black woman is directed away from a waiting room for whites at a bus station.*

Who Worked to Make the Holiday?

Dr. King was shot and killed in 1968. Four days later, Michigan Congressman John Conyers asked that a holiday be named for Dr. King.

Coretta Scott King, Dr. King's wife, later started the Martin Luther King Jr. Memorial Center in Atlanta. Mrs. King, members of the memorial center staff, and many other Americans also asked the **federal** government to create the holiday. The government said no, but the people kept asking. During the next 15 years, some states observed Dr. King's birthday, but many did not.

◄ *People clap for Coretta Scott King on Martin Luther King Jr. Day in Atlanta.*

Did Everyone Like the New Holiday?

In 1983, President Ronald Reagan signed a bill that made Martin Luther King Jr. Day a national holiday. The bill said the first event would be in 1986.

Not everyone liked the idea of making a holiday for Dr. King. Some believed other Americans deserved a holiday before Dr. King. Others thought the holiday should honor the whole civil rights movement, not one of its leaders.

Some people felt the new holiday was too close to Christmas and New Year's Day. Business owners worried they would lose money by giving their employees another day off.

◀ *President Reagan signs a paper making Martin Luther King Jr. Day a national holiday.*

How Is Martin Luther King Jr. Day Observed?

Some places celebrate Martin Luther King Jr. Day with parades or marches. Others have quiet services to remember him. People also give speeches about Dr. King, the civil rights movement, freedom, and peace. The largest celebrations are held in Dr. King's hometown, Atlanta, Georgia.

Dr. King helped others his whole life. Many feel that Martin Luther King Jr. Day should be spent doing the same thing. On this special day, people **volunteer** to do good deeds. They paint schools, clean up litter, and deliver food to the elderly. Some say this holiday is "a day on, not a day off."

◄ People march for peace on Martin Luther King Jr. Day.

COMMUNITY BANK WHEATON/GLEN ELLYN

Community Bank
Wheaton/Glen Ellyn

Will be *Closed*
Monday
January 19, 2004

in Commemoration of
Martin Luther King, Jr.

Please drive carefully and have a
Safe & Happy Holiday!

	Lobby	Drive-Up
MON.-FRI.	8:30 to 5:30	7:00 to 8:00
SATURDAY	8:30 to 1:00	

Where Is Martin Luther King Jr. Day Observed?

Martin Luther King Jr. Day is celebrated in all 50 states and Washington, D.C. Schools, post offices, banks, federal offices, and some companies close for this holiday.

Americans living around the world celebrate as well. People in more than 100 nations observe Martin Luther King Jr. Day in some way. Some countries, including the Caribbean island country of Trinidad and Tobago, have their own holidays to remember Dr. King.

◄ *A sign on a bank door says the bank will be closed for Martin Luther King Jr. Day.*

What Is Special About Martin Luther King Jr. Day?

In the United States, Dr. King is only the third person to have his own national holiday. The others honored are George Washington and Christopher Columbus. Dr. King is the first black person to be honored with a holiday that is celebrated all across the country.

Martin Luther King Jr. Day was the third and final major holiday the U.S. government created in the 20th century. The others were Veterans Day and Presidents' Day.

◄ *Martin and Coretta sit with three of their four children at their home in 1968.*

What Does the Holiday Mean to People?

Martin Luther King Jr. Day means different things to different people. To some, it is a day to think about Dr. King's life. To others, it is a day to remember the civil rights movement.

On Martin Luther King Jr. Day, people are reminded that racism still exists. There is still work to do to make sure all people are treated fairly.

Martin Luther King Jr. Day is a day for all people to celebrate. It is a good time to notice that people's differences are beautiful, and that people are the same in a lot of ways, too.

◄ *Friends give each other a high five.*

Glossary

civil rights movement—in the 1950s and 1960s, an effort to gain African-Americans equal treatment in the United States

discrimination—treating people unfairly because of their race, religion, sex, or age

federal—having to do with the nation

racism—the belief that one race is better than others

segregation—keeping people of different races apart

volunteer—to offer to do something without being paid

Did You Know?

* Some states have called Martin Luther King Jr. Day by another name. Utah has called it Human Rights Day. New Hampshire used to call it Civil Rights Day.

* The first time Martin Luther King Jr. Day was celebrated in all 50 states was in 1999. New Hampshire was the last state to make it an official holiday.

* Martin Luther King Jr. won the Nobel Peace Prize in 1964. He earned this big honor by using peaceful ways to make changes happen.

* Because he did so well in high school, Martin Luther King Jr. was able to skip two grades. He was 15 years old when he started college.

* Martin Luther King Jr. has been honored in many other ways. Monuments and memorials have been built for him. Libraries, hospitals, parks, and streets are named after him. His image has been on postage stamps in many countries.

Want to Know More?

In the Library

Marx, David F. *Martin Luther King Jr. Day.* New York: Children's Press, 2001.

Nettleton, Pamela Hill. *Martin Luther King Jr.: Preacher, Freedom Fighter, Peacemaker.* Minneapolis: Picture Window Books, 2004.

Raatma, Lucia. *Martin Luther King Jr.* Minneapolis: Compass Point Books, 2002.

Rau, Dana Meachen. *Martin Luther King Jr. Day.* New York.: Children's Press, 2001.

On the Web

For more information on *Martin Luther King Jr.,* use FactHound to track down Web sites related to this book.

1. Go to *www.facthound.com*
2. Type in a search word related to this book or this book ID: 0756506468.
3. Click on the *Fetch It* button.

Your trusty FactHound will fetch the best Web sites for you!

On the Road

Martin Luther King Jr. National Historic Site
450 Auburn Ave. N.E.
Atlanta, GA 30312-1525
404/331-5190
To see a video about Dr. King's life and exhibits about the civil rights movement

The King Center
449 Auburn Ave. N.E.
Atlanta, GA 30312
404/526-8900
To visit exhibits in the Freedom Hall and learn more about Dr. King

Index

Atlanta, Georgia, 5, 11, 15
buses, 7
civil rights movement, 5, 13, 15, 21
Columbus, Christopher, 19
Conyers, John, 11
date, 5, 13
discrimination, 7
King, Coretta Scott, 11
King, Martin Luther, Jr., 5, 7, 9, 11, 19, 21
marches, 15
Martin Luther King Jr. Memorial Center, 11
Montgomery, Alabama, 7
parades, 15
racism, 5, 21
Reagan, Ronald, 13
schools, 9
segregation, 7, 9
speeches, 15
states, 11, 17
Supreme Court, 7
Trinidad and Tobago, 17
Veterans Day, 19
volunteers, 15
Washington, George, 19

About the Author

Marc Tyler Nobleman has written more than 40 books for young readers. He has also written for a History Channel show called "The Great American History Quiz" and for several children's magazines including *Nickelodeon, Highlights for Children,* and *Read* (a Weekly Reader publication). He is also a cartoonist, and his single panels have appeared in more than 100 magazines internationally. He lives in Connecticut.